YOU CAN BE A WOMAN ™ ANIMATOR

Judith Love Cohen

With contributions from Vicky Jenson, MaryAnn Malcomb, Claire Morrissey, Cathy Jones, Michelle Cowart, and Kathy Zielinski

Editing:
Lee Rathbone

Cascade
Pass, Inc.

www.cascadepass.com

Copyright © 2004 by Cascade Pass, Inc.
Published by Cascade Pass, Inc., Suite C-105
4223 Glencoe Avenue
Marina del Rey, CA 90292-8801
Phone (310) 305-0210
Printed in Hong Kong by South China Printing Co. (1988) Ltd.

You Can Be a Woman Animator was written by Judith Love Cohen with contributions from animators: Vicky Jenson, MaryAnn Malcomb, Claire Morrissey, Cathy Jones, Michelle Cowart, and Kathy Zielinski, Art Director David Katz, and edited by Lee Rathbone. Graphics design by Kana Tatekawa of Momo Communications, Inc. Shark Tale™ © 2004 graphic material supplied by DreamWorks, L.L.C.

This book is one of a series that emphasizes the value of art and other non-traditional careers by depicting real women whose careers provide inspirational role models.

Other recent books in the series include:

You Can Be A Woman Architect

You Can Be A Woman Paleontologist

You Can Be A Woman Zoologist

You Can Be A Woman Soccer Player

You Can Be A Woman Movie Maker

You Can Be A Woman Meteorologist

You Can Be A Woman Oceanographer

You Can Be A Woman Egyptologist

You Can Be A Woman Entomologist

You Can Be A Woman Botanist

You Can Be A Woman Marine Biologist

You Can Be A Woman Engineer

You Can Be A Woman Softball Player

You Can Be A Woman Basketball Player

Library of Congress Cataloging-in-Publication Data

Cohen, Judith Love, 1933-
    You can be a woman animator / Judith Love Cohen; with contributions from Vicky Jenson [et al.]. – 1st ed.
        p.   cm.
    ISBN 1-880599-69-4 (pbk.) – ISBN 1-880599-70-8 (hard cover)
    1. Computer animation. I. Jenson, Vicky. II. Title.
TR897.5.C64 2004
791.43'34–dc22   2004007806

Dedication

This book is dedicated by author Judith Love Cohen to her son, Jack, whose first award was for an animation he did in high school.

This book is dedicated by contributor Vicky Jenson to her mom and dad who always encouraged her to pursue creativity, happiness, and social contribution in art.

This book is dedicated by contributor Cathy Jones to her mother, Shirley Dwyer, who always told her she could do anything or be anything she wanted to be.

This book is dedicated by contributor MaryAnn Malcolm to her mother Marjorie, a terrific artist, her biggest fan and her greatest inspiration.

This book is dedicated by contributor Claire Morrissey to her kids, Nathan and Liana.

This book is dedicated by contributor Michelle Cowart to her parents Dan and Betty and to her friend Steve.

This book is dedicated by contributor Kathy Zielinski to her daughters Jennifer and Allison.

It's a bright sunny morning in Glendale, CA, as Vicky Jenson comes running into the building a little out of breath. She relaxes a bit as she looks at the clock. "Almost on time!" she says gleefully to the receptionist as she hurries up the steps to her office. But she just drops off her purse and rushes down the hall to the Editing Department, where the movie is taking shape, sequence by sequence.

Today, Vicky and the editors review an animation sequence. Vicky squints as she watches the scene. "That's supposed to be a joyous smile and it looks more like a sneer." She makes a note. "MaryAnn, could you try another version of Lenny's expression?"

In another sequence, the editors have added dialogue and sound effects to an action sequence. "That sounded fine separately from the visuals, but they don't sound right together. I like the action. I'll see if we can get Will back to re-record those lines of dialogue to sound as if he's swimming fast to match the action." And she makes another note.

In front of another computer down the hall, MaryAnn Malcomb is loading up the scene she has been working on all week. The job of an animator like MaryAnn is to create the expressions and the movements that will bring the scene to life. To make this easy, the programmers have provided many handles on everything, from eyebrows to toes. MaryAnn is busy with the mouth today. That smile needs more work.

And close by, in front of yet another computer, Claire Morrissey is working on the same sequence. She is dealing with the characters just before the part that MaryAnn is working on. She reviews the notes that Vicky, the director, has made. Claire is imagining a different pose for the character based on Vicky's comments.

And Cathy Jones, another animator, is starting to work on a new sequence. She is reviewing the storyboards and acting out the scene in her head. "How do I make this character come alive?"

Michelle Cowart is another animator working on some of the same characters that Cathy is. Sometime earlier, character designers have created the computer representations of the characters as modeled. This is what the animators are manipulating.

And Kathy Zielinski is reviewing the scene segments and checking for continuity and appropriate character acting. She is watching the live action reference tapes of one of the voice talents for expressions or acting ideas. She will make printouts of the frame or maybe draw the expressions to take back to her desk to look at while she's animating the scene. She might also listen to the voice track and look at the exposure sheet to determine what type of action to animate and exactly where in the scene the action will occur.

While all of these professionals see themselves as being a part of a team, and working together like members of a symphony orchestra to create something beautiful and harmonious, the fact of the matter is that animation is, and always has been, lonely work. For many of their working hours, they will sit by themselves with visions dancing in their heads and on the screens.

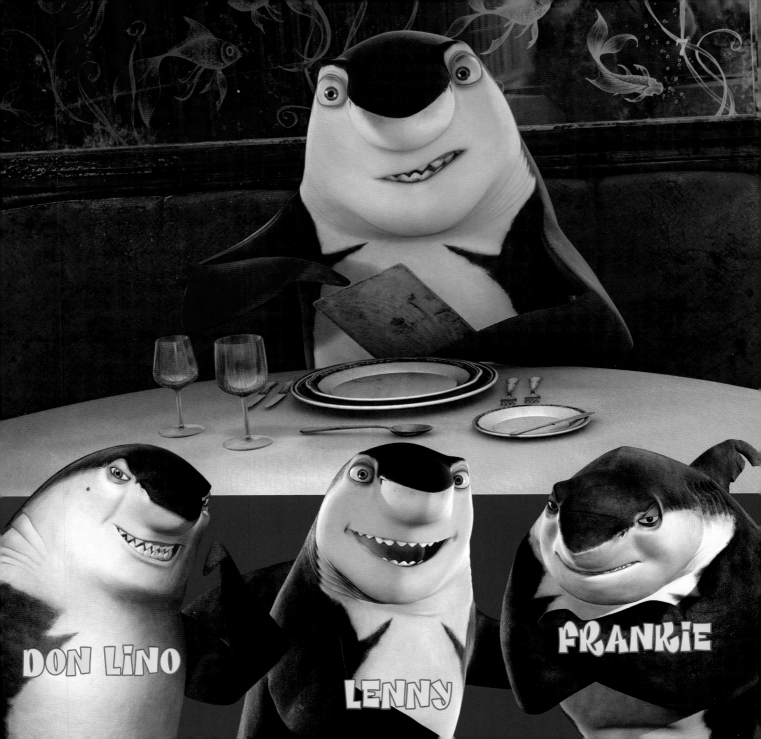

DON LINO

LENNY

FRANKIE

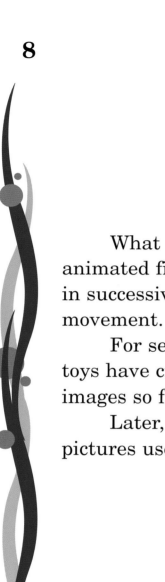

What is animation? Usually, "animation" refers to animated films. Animated films are made up of drawings in successive positions that can have the illusion of movement.

For several hundred years, mechanical and optical toys have created this illusion by spinning or projecting images so fast that your eye sees motion.

Later, photography was invented and moving pictures used the same devices and toys and projectors.

But animation, an American art, involves drawing in a special way. The characters have gestures and expressions that invest them with personality and emotions. The animator is "acting with a pencil" and dramatizing and making visual the characters' thoughts and reactions in an entertaining and engaging way.

The animation process starts with screenwriting: a script, plot, and dialogue. The script then needs to be expressed in visuals: the action, the expressions, and the colors are created through storyboards, character design, background design, character animation, and lighting. The audio portion: music, dialogue, and sound effects are created and mixed in with visuals.

10

sykes

Cathy Jones working on facial expression

So these women animators are part of an old tradition. But where did these women animators come from? What was their childhood like? Vicky Jenson was born and grew up in the San Fernando Valley in California. She was an active youngster climbing trees, riding her bike, gardening, and dancing ballet.

In school she liked a lot of her classes, including algebra, physics, Spanish, orchestra, and the common denominator, art. She drew pictures all her life.

Michelle Cowart, from Bradenton, Florida, spent a lot of time at the beach, a typical pursuit followed by young Floridians. She also was a cartoonist for the school newspaper and her mural, painted on a section of a wall, won an award. Painting and drawing were her passions. Drawing caricatures of friends and family was a favorite pasttime.

MaryAnn Malcomb, from Ventura, CA, while indulging in activities such as horseback riding and reading, created her own comic strip at the age of 11 and "drew all the time."

Cathy Jones was born in Boston, MA, and moved to California with her folks when she was fifteen. And similarly, while Cathy liked to read, she also used the words on the page to stir the visual images she would imagine; she also "drew every day."

Cathy Jones

Michelle Cowart

MaryAnn Malcomb

Kathy Zielinski is another California "beach" girl, but after a day at the beach, gymnastics or sports, she would always "sit down and draw." She didn't imagine that she would be able to make a living as an artist, so initially, she was preparing for a medical career after high school.

Luckily, in her senior year her art teacher, Mr. James Pickard, offered a class in animation. Kathy was not in that class at first, but when she saw what they were doing, she immediately transferred over.

Claire Morrissey's background was very different. Growing up in Montreal, Canada, she spent time playing in the snow and sledding before picking up her pen to draw.

Claire Morrissey

Vicky Jenson

Kathy Zielinski

How did these animators make their career choices? What led them to this special work?

While someone may have a native talent for ice skating or for playing the violin, unless they have an opportunity to try out the ice or hold the instrument, they may never realize that talent.

But artists, from the first time they hold a pencil or a crayon, can sense the possibility in their very own hands. All of these women knew that they could draw and enjoyed doing it from a young age. But how to translate that ability into a career choice?

A person with a talent for art has many career options. She can be a book illustrator, comic strip artist, cartoonist, or graphics artist for advertising or web design. She can create sets or backgrounds for theater, or live action or animated films. She can also design characters or be an animator in animated films.

All of our animators went to art school; five of them right after high school and one later, after considering a different career.

And at DreamWorks, where they are animators, they have different roles. But let's talk about the animation process so we can see where all of this fits in.

We talked about what animation is, now let's talk about how we do it.

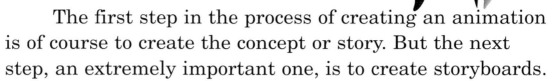

The first step in the process of creating an animation is of course to create the concept or story. But the next step, an extremely important one, is to create storyboards.

A storyboard is a collected series of single pictures. A storyboard is created for each visual sequence within the project. Agreeing on a storyboard is a vital step in the animation process.

As the storyboard captures the action in the visual sequences, conceptual artists are defining a preliminary look of the final project: characters, sets, colors, and lighting, are captured in sketches, paintings, and clay models.

Meetings among writers, director, and artists result in agreement on the details of the action and the look of the characters.

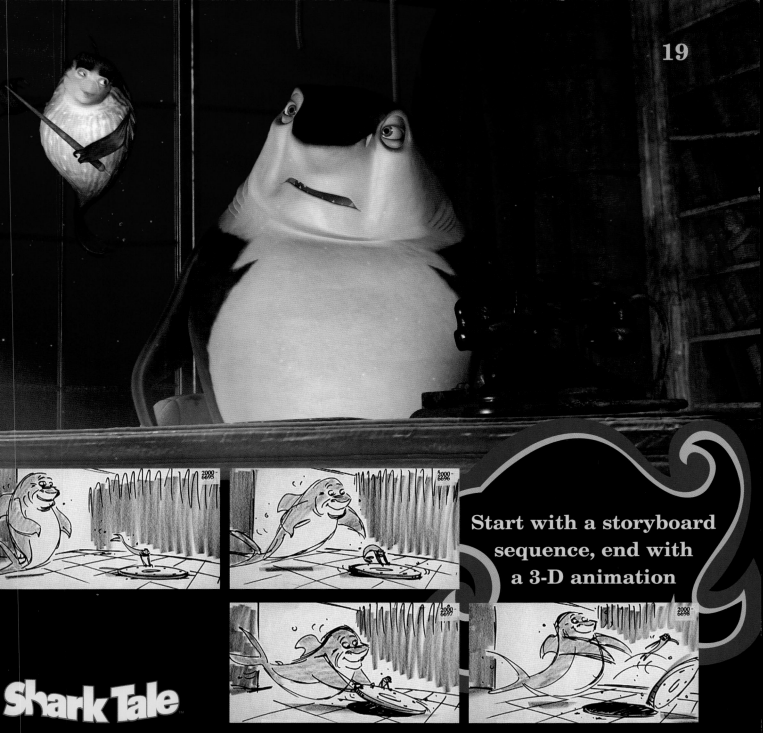

Start with a storyboard sequence, end with a 3-D animation

Shark Tale

The next step depends on which comes first: the sound track (voice-over) or the visuals.

Often the actors record the sound track first and they are videotaped, so the animators can use the video for timing and facial expressions. In the early days, the animation was done first and the dialogue was added later.

OSCAR

ANGIE

The backgrounds will be created in 3-D with lighting and colors. The characters may be modeled in clay or hand-drawn. But ultimately the character design is captured in a computer. Handles and controls are added so that animators have the control required to add expressive and subtle movements and lip sync.

Finally, animators work on specific characters, adding the motion and subtle details to bring the characters to life. Then the editors and sound effects, music, and dialogue are added to the visual tracks, and we have a feature.

Clay models help in
character design

Vicky Jenson has been directing DreamWorks' *Shark Tale*™ for the past three and a half years. It is in the final stages: editing, adding music, and fine-tuning. Vicky's role as director has involved a lot of different kinds of work, from working with the writers and storyboard artists to develop the conceptual look and tone of the film, to dealing with lighting and color gels and even makeup for the characters.

Of course, the director works with the actors and then the animators to make sure they are creating a scene that is in harmony with the overall vision. Vicky is like the conductor of a symphony orchestra, where each member's instrument must be in harmony with the rest of the orchestra, and they all must follow the conductor's direction.

Vicky's career led from painting cels for a family member's commercials while babysitting, to painting backgrounds, to storyboarding films as a summer job that didn't end.

Vicky Jenson,
director,
in recording
studio

So far, she considers her directing contribution on *Shrek*™, working with Mike Myers, Eddie Murphy, and Cameron Diaz to be her best completed work, and its reception by people everywhere as her proudest achievement.

While she's extremely proud of her work on *Shrek*™ and how it reached people everywhere, Vicky is finding *Shark Tale*™ to be even more creatively rewarding. It is offering even more of a opportunity to work with actors in creating their characters. Will Smith, Robert De Niro, Martin Scorsese, Jack Black, Angelina Jolie, and Renée Zellweger, among others, have contributed to the creation of the characters by recording and video-taping the dialogue, thus allowing the character design and animation to reflect the actor's interpretation and the irector's vision.

Lenny

Jack Black,
actor,
in recording
studio

28

Vicky particularly enjoys working with actors and in an animation of this type, there is a lot of similarity to the director's interaction in a live action film.

Vicky dreams of directing a live action film or a play, where her interaction with the actors would be more immediate and intense.

Kathy Zielinski has been an animator at DreamWorks for a number of different animated films, and on *Shark Tale*™ is working on the animation of five different characters.

She always loved the animation films of Disney and realized that she could try to get a job there. She sent a portfolio over to California Institute of Arts in Valencia, and at first she was told that her work was not good enough but if she wanted she could submit a second portfolio. She did and got in!

Kathy Zielinski,
animator

OSCAR

LENNY

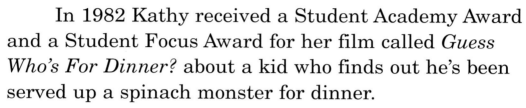

In 1982 Kathy received a Student Academy Award and a Student Focus Award for her film called *Guess Who's For Dinner?* about a kid who finds out he's been served up a spinach monster for dinner.

She went on to work for Disney as an animator and character designer on films such as *Pocahontas* and *The Hunchback of Notre Dame*. She was a supervisor on *The Rescuer's Down Under*.

Kathy joined DreamWorks as a supervisor of the villain "Tzekel-Kan" for *The Road to El Dorado*.

Kathy Zielinski,
animator

Kathy's biggest achievement was in designing the character "Frollo" in *The Hunchback of Notre Dame*. She was one of the rare women to be a lead animator at Disney. Her goals include making independent films with her husband.

Michelle Cowart has been a 3-D animator at DreamWorks since they created their first animated feature. Before *Shark Tale*™, she did 3-D character animation in five animated features. When the 3-D computer animation department was small, she helped with modeling the character, building the wire skeleton, adding skin, defining the lighting, and finally rendering. Now she is focused on doing the animation.

Michelle Cowart,
animator

Michelle was the cartoonist for her school newspaper. She majored in computer animation at Ringling School in Sarasota, Florida. Although she initially felt most comfortable drawing illustrations and doing sculpture by hand, she learned to overcome the technological challenges and use computer programs instead.

Michelle is most proud of her character animation in *Shark Tale*™ scenes involving Robert De Niro's great white shark character. Michelle dreams of doing more of this full-character animation – creating dialogue and expressions, and working on scenes. As with all artists, she looks forward to seeing her work receive good audience reaction.

ERNIE & Bernie

"DON'LAND"

Michelle Cowart, animator

CHILLS MY GILLS YO!

Cathy Jones is now working on her first computer-generated feature animation, *Shark Tale*™. She previously worked on three traditionally animated films at DreamWorks, starting with *The Prince of Egypt*, where she did visual development and then animation.

Cathy's career choices always involved art. She drew every day from the time she was 3 or 4, but usually she visualized herself as a book illustrator, a graphics designer, or an art director. Her first animation job was assistant animator on the original *An American Tail*. She became an animator two years later while working and living in Dublin, Ireland.

In addition to animation, she did visual development and storyboards at various studios, including MGM, before coming to DreamWorks.

Cathy Jones,
animator

MaryAnn Malcomb,
animator

Cathy's proudest achievement was her work on PBS's *Roman City*. Her storyboards, character design, and direction resulted in an Emmy for this film. Her goal is to direct the animations and add to the stories.

MaryAnn Malcomb is working as an animator on *Shark Tale*™, where she does the dialogue and characters in a scene. She also is working on a scene involving Oscar, a cleaner wrasse fish (brilliantly colored, long, slender fish that buries itself in the sand at night) voiced by Will Smith, and Lenny, a great white shark voiced by Jack Black.

Although she "drew all the time," had a comic strip at 10, and once wanted to be a cartoonist for a newspaper, she graduated from UC Davis with a degree in international relations and went to live in Taiwan to learn Mandarin. Somehow she had decided that art was not a "proper" career.

MaryAnn Malcomb,
animator

Although MaryAnn loved the adventure of living in another country, she soon realized how much she missed art. She decided to go back to school, to California Institute of Arts to be exact, and began her career as a character layout artist on TV shows such as *The Simpsons* and *The Critic*. Mary Ann came to DreamWorks and worked on four animations before *Shark Tale*™.

Her proudest achievement, aside from being a new parent, was her first job on *The Simpsons*. She wanted to do her very best, but she worried that maybe she wouldn't be good enough. She gripped her pencil so hard while she drew that she got blisters on her fingers! After a few months, it was a wonderful feeling when the directors complimented her work and wanted to work with her again.

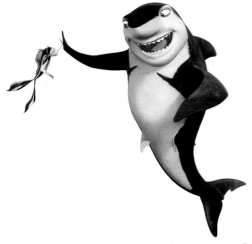

MaryAnn is also very proud of her work as a lead animator on *Spirit: Stallion of the Cimarron*. She got to help design and then animate the little girl that pulls "Spirit's nostrils."

Her goals include writing and illustrating children's books and working on independent films.

Claire Morrissey is working as an animator on *Shark Tale*™ where she uses the dialogue and characters in the scene immediately preceding MaryAnn's. Claire and MaryAnn also are working on a smooth transition from one scene to the next. It wouldn't do to have Oscar facing left at the end of Claire's scene and facing right at the start MaryAnn's scene.

Claire Morrissey,
animator

Claire grew up in Montreal, Canada. Her grandmother had been a medical illustrator and her aunt worked as a professional artist. Following their example, Claire studied film and art, took drawing classes, and spent a lot of time at the park and the zoo drawing people and animals. Her first job after art college (Sheridan college) was as a character designer. She went on to work as an animator for Warner Brothers and Disney.

Claire's proudest moment was on her first film. She had been hired as an assistant, but had animated a scene on her own, using one of the characters from the movie. She felt really nervous about showing it to the director, but when he saw the scene he liked it and promoted her from assistant to animator! Claire's goals are to write her own story and illustrate it, make her own short animation movie, and lead a team of actors in a sequence of scenes.

Claire Morrissey
acting out
a part

DON LINO

How can you tell if you would be good at animation? If you can answer yes to the following questions, then you should consider being an animator.

1. *Do you like to draw?*
   Do you find yourself doing it a lot?

   Animators love to draw, and they spend a lot of time working at it. "Talent is overrated; 90% is willingness to work, and 10% is talent," said one of our animators.

2. *Do you love movement and acting?*
   Do you see yourself as an entertainer?

   Our animators describe themselves as "a little bit of a ham" or "entertainers." Drawing cartoons or characters can be seen as "acting with a pencil."

OSCAR

LENNY

Vicky Jenson,
director, working
with editor,
Nick Fletcher

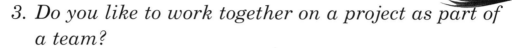

3. *Do you like to work together on a project as part of a team?*

   Can you communicate and cooperate with others?

   A few minutes of animation can take a few months to draw by hand or a few weeks to create on a computer. Obviously, a feature-length animation takes a number of animators working together. As part of a team there are two important qualities: persistence and flexibility. While those seem to conflict, it's part of a good interaction. People should be flexible enough to listen to good ideas from others but persistent enough to hold onto their own ideas if they believe in them.

Shark Tale™
Concept Art

4. *Can you visualize something in your head, see the "big picture"?*

Each small animation sequence must fit into a larger context and each animator needs to understand how her sequence fits in.

Shark Tale
Concept Art

If you want to be an animator, you will need to develop three things: 1. Your hands; 2. your eyes; 3. your brain.

1. Your hands should always be drawing – doodling, caricaturing, or sketching. Keep your sketchpad with you and don't be afraid to fill it up!!

2. Your eyes need to learn to observe. Is that frown caused by hunger or sadness or…? How does that cat move when it is sneaking up on a mouse or when it is chasing a bird?

3. Your brain can be used to study stories, movies, plays, and television. What makes a good story? What makes these actors' performances live? What makes the scene so real or surreal?

If you truly love to draw "all the time," if you just love "acting" in many forms, and if you enjoy sharing your work with a talented team, then you can do it too! You Can Be A Woman Animator.

YOU CAN BE A WOMAN ANIMATOR

ANIMATOR LESSON PLAN 1

PURPOSE: To gain an understanding of how still pictures get to move, or the "flip book" principle.

MATERIALS: Clear white pads of paper, watercolor markers, black pens or markers.

PROCEDURES: Have the children each take a pad of paper and a pen or marker.
Have them start on the last page and draw a circle on one side of the page. Draw the same circle on the next page forward, and have it move toward the center. Draw the circle moving in successive drawings toward the other side of the page.
Then have it bounce back to the original side.
Flip the pages of the book to see the movement of the circle.
If the children have more time, have them repeat this with an animal or a person walking across the page.

CONCLUSIONS: Does your sequence of drawings appear to move? What effect does it have if it crosses the page in fewer drawings? In more drawings?

ANIMATOR LESSON PLAN 2

PURPOSE: To understand how cartoons capture a likeness, or "caricature."

MATERIALS: Pencils, pads of paper.

PROCEDURES: Have children form pairs. One child gets a pencil and pad. The other child makes a face, or a gesture, or talks or chews gum, or some kind of action. The first child studies the face of her partner and draws the expression, exaggerating the specific features they see. Have the children reverse and the other children do the same.
The children can draw a single picture first and if they get the idea of focusing on a particular feature and depicting it, they can do a sequence of drawings, changing the feature slightly in each drawing.

CONCLUSIONS: What features did you choose to portray? Were the different children's drawings unique? What made them different from each other?

ANIMATOR LESSON PLAN 3

PURPOSE: Learn how important observation can be.

MATERIALS: Pad and pencil.

PROCEDURES: Think of a place you like to go: park, schoolyard, patio, or cafeteria. Have the children pick one place to go to "observe."

Have the children sit and look around at the things that are normally there: flowers blowing in the breeze, ants crawling on the ground, birds flying, and most important, people. Have the children observe how people move: arms, shoulders, and legs, when they are walking or eating or sitting down.

Have the children pick an interesting person or animal to sketch and have them note particular gestures. Have them scribble with lines; details are not important, the feeling of the movement is what is important.

CONCLUSIONS: What kind of feelings do your sketches try to convey? Is the movement big and bold or subtle and delicate?

Can you translate these sketches into a series of drawings that actually capture the motion? What gestures help you to do this?

ANIMATOR LESSON PLAN 4

PURPOSE: Develop an understanding of how the camera helps to tell a story.

MATERIALS: TV set, paper, marker pens, poster board, watch with second hand.

PROCEDURES: Have the class watch a TV show with the sound turned off. Have them time the length of the shots, and observe the different kinds of shots: close-ups, or panning shots for example. (Refer to the Nomenclature for the names of different kinds of shots.)

Have each child draw one of the children from a different angle and distance. Place several of these on the poster board in successive pictures. Have one child make up a story about the pictures.

Jumble the pictures and select a different set in a different order. Have another child make up a story about these pictures.

CONCLUSIONS: How does the angle of the camera or the distance influence what you see?
How much does the camera move in a scene of only a few minutes?

ANIMATOR LESSON PLAN 5

PURPOSE: Develop an understanding of how lighting affects the scene.

MATERIALS: Large cardboard box, basketball, two small point lights, colored cellophane: orange, yellow, blue.

PROCEDURES: Cut the top and the front off the box so it's like a small stage. Put the basketball in the middle.
Have a child hold the light in several different positions: shining down on the basketball, lighting from the front, from one side, and from behind.
Have another child take the second light and move it through the different positions, taking different positions than the first light, so we have combinations like light on top, light from the back, etc.
Repeat with cellophane over the lights to give them colors.

CONCLUSIONS: What kind of feelings do you get from the different lighting arrangements? How is the mood changed when you change the colors of the lights?
Which lighting setup did you like the best? What feeling (warm, scary, mysterious, exciting) did it convey?

ANIMATOR LESSON PLAN 6

PURPOSE: To gain an understanding of how animation goes from a script to a storyboard to an animated sequence.

MATERIALS: Copy of a few pages from a play or a cartoon, glue, scissors, marker pens, construction paper, cardboard, and masking tape.

PROCEDURES: Have the children read the play or cartoon aloud and decide what movements the characters will have (e.g., picking up a spoon, answering the telephone).

Have them list the different shots that will be required to capture the action of the scene. Assign each child one or two shot drawings. Have them draw the action, using as much perspective as they can. Cut out the drawings and mount on construction paper.

Have the children arrange the individual shots as a storyboard (like a comic strip, in sequence). The storyboard translates the story into pictures.

CONCLUSIONS: What did you choose to put into the storyboard that wasn't in the words? Why?

ANIMATOR LESSON PLAN 7

PURPOSE: Practice acting and directing without using words, such as pantomime, or silent films.

MATERIALS: Several copies of a storyboard as in lesson plan 4, pens, paper.

PROCEDURES: Choose a director. Choose classmates to play different parts.
Have the director work with the actors, and help them use gestures, movement, and exaggeration to express the part.
Do the scene.
Choose a different director and cast members.
Repeat the work and the scene.
Have the class discuss the different versions and how they saw the interactions.

CONCLUSIONS: Was the scene done the same both times? How did it differ, and why did it happen?
Now that the class has acted out the part, how would they change the drawings or storyboard to fit the new version of the character?

ANIMATOR LESSON PLAN 8

PURPOSE: To understand animation about non-specific objects or abstraction.

MATERIALS: Toys, objects such as wooden cubes, still camera, or video camera.

PROCEDURES: Lay out some of the objects on the floor in some order or arrangement. Take pictures of the arrangement.
Have the children move the objects and then take another picture. Make sure that the arms and hands of those moving the objects are not in the frame of the picture. Move the objects at least 20 to 25 times.
Once it is filmed, play the pictures back in sequence, forward or backward. Play music if available.

CONCLUSIONS: How do you feel when you see the objects move? How can you make the experience more meaningful or interesting in the playback? What about different music, different speed, different light, different colors and textures?

ANIMATOR LESSON PLAN 9 (ADVANCED)

PURPOSE: To try to model an object on a 3-D computer program.

MATERIALS: Computer with 3-D modeling program that allows you to select objects such as a cube, sphere, or cone.

PROCEDURES: Have each child take a turn at the computer doing the lesson.
Start by selecting a cube and stretch it in length so it is like a plank of wood. Now stretch it in width so it is like the top of a dinner table. Rotate the table top so you can look at the bottom. Add a small cube to the bottom of the table. Stretch the cube in height so that it will be a center support for the table. Next add a bigger cube at the end of the support. Stretch this out so that it can form a base for the table. Rotate the table so that it can now stand on its base.

CONCLUSIONS: What do we mean by 3-D? (Three dimensional)

Nomenclature

anti-aliasing: a process of blurring sharp edges in pictures to get rid of the jagged edges on lines. After an image is rendered, some applications automatically anti-alias images. The program looks for edges in an image, and then blurs adjacent pixels to produce a smoother edge.

bones: an actual skeletal system you set up to help control movement realistically and to keep things in order. An outline for you to base the rest of the shapes of the objects on.

Boolean: in order to create a Boolean object, you first need two other objects. They can be primitives or other meshes. They also need to intersect in 3-D space. If you do addition, the resulting object will be the sum of the two initial objects. It will look as if the two were welded. If substation is what you are doing, the second object gets subtracted from the first one. A hole in the shape of the second object is created in the first one. All the space that was occupied by both of the objects is taken away from the first one. Finally, in the intersection mode, the final object occupies the area in which both of the initial intersected.

CAD/CAM: the abbreviation for Computer Aided Design/Computer Aided Manufacturing, a combination of CAD and CAM. For example, a designer creates a 3-dimensional representation of an object, with the help of the computer, and then the computer programs instructions for automated manufacture of the object and controls the manufacturing process.

camera: the camera serves as an object through which to view the other objects of the scene. You can have more than one, and probably should do so. Cameras are hugely important in how you want to present or show your talent. A creative perspective can turn an ordinary block into so much more.

caricature: a picture or other figure or description in which the peculiarities of a person or thing are so exaggerated as to appear ridiculous.

cel: a special plastic sheet animators use in the final stages of a developed frame to allow a static background to surround the object without much hassle.

CGI: stands for computer generated imagery, creating moving images through the use of computers. 3-D computer graphics are distinct from 2-D computer graphics in that a three-dimensional virtual representation of objects is stored in the computer for the purposes of performing calculations and rendering images.

close-up: a shot where the subject fills up most of the frame, if shooting a person, then it is their head and shoulders.

concept sketch: a key frame of animation in a scene, or an idea for a design for the animation.

exposure sheet: a place mark sheet where every individual element in the film that is animated can be layered on separate sheets.

extreme close-up: a shot where the screen is filled with just the subject's face.

falloff: referring to light sources, a spot where the light hits the object.

flip book: a sequence of small sheets of paper to draw the frames on quickly. You then flip with your thumbnail to check if the animation looks right, works right, and if it speaks the scene well.

frame: a single picture to be used in a single animation scene. A cartoon shows at about 24 frames a second. That's about 35, 000 frames for a 30 minute episode.

Giclee: an extremely high-resolution digital image of the artist's original artwork, loaded into specially enhanced printers, which output the digital image onto fine art paper or canvas. Since the digital image includes every subtlety and nuance of the original – including the smallest details of light and shadow such as the textures of the paint and canvas or paper – the fine art giclee is often indistinguishable from the original work of art. Brush strokes have the appearance of brush strokes, even though they are only two-dimensional images on paper. Typically, limited edition artwork is hand-signed by the artist indicating their personal approval of each work of art, then individually numbered to identify each work of art as a part of the total edition.

handles: are the control points in a 3-D scene used to manipulate the object for rotating, moving, and scaling.

horizon: a line in the background of the scene that serves as the focus point upon which all foreground items will be related to.

in-between: an image drawn to show a character between the extreme moments of action or gesture.

key: an important factor in the animation part of the project. Each key you create stands for the beginning and the end of each separate action you wish to instill in the object. This is a HUGE step up in user-friendliness, as opposed to the old ways of animating things frame by frame like a cartoon. It's a lot more orderly too. Let's say you put a key at 10 seconds into the film. This key could now stand for the end of an action that started from 0 second, and if you add another key 2 seconds later, this key can stand for beginning of a whole new one. And in between these keys you can do SO MUCH at one time it's so sweet.

keyframe: an individual image exhibiting the extreme of an action or gesture.

lithograph: a print made using a traditional printing process whereby the artist's original image is transferred onto stone or metal lithography plates, usually by hand, or chemically. Each color must be separated from the original image, then transferred to the stone or plate. Under very heavy pressure, each color is printed onto fine art paper, one color at a time. When all of the image's individual colors have been printed together onto the paper, the combined colors create the final and complete art. Typically, limited edition lithographs are hand-signed by the artist indicating their personal approval of each work of art, then individually numbered to identify each lithograph as a part of the total edition.

Lofted object: two things: a shape, and a line/track telling it how to form into a 3-D shape. The shape is used for the base of what the object is going to look like if you were to take a cross-section of it. The line is used to tell that shape to follow along its path and create a whole new 3-D one in the process. The Lofting tool allows different shaped profiles on different elevations to be connected to form a solid object. The resulting shape can be altered after lofting by modifying the individual profiles. The 2-D profiles are connected using NURB calculations.

material: the texture you want to put on any certain object. For a tree, use a grainy, wood material, and the foliage can be a grassy material, stretched out. Materials are important to add a huge amount of realism to the scene. Without materials the scene just really isn't much fun to look at. What would a paved road be without a few loose pebbles, or craggy holes? Think of that same road gray, blank, bland. Looks as slippery as a gym floor, which is not right. See? Materials are what give objects a real-world look. Things would look way too much like toys without them.

medium shot: a shot where the subject and some background are on the screen. Shoot a person from the waist up.

mesh: a collection of faces which describe an object. An object can be anything, a sphere, a pyramid, a car tire, or an elephant. The faces are arranged in such a way that they form the outside surface of that object. It could be thought of as the skin of the object. The mesh is usually depicted in wireframe mode, as this shows the faces and the outline and does not take very long to render.

metamorphosis: a clay animation technique in which one character is transformed into another by gradually re-sculpting the figure.

motion capture: a very expensive alternative to the hassle of controlling every aspect of object animation. The object to be animated is pre-created just like normal but then the producers bring a real human or animal in, strap a whole bunch of infrared sensors to keypoints where animation has been studied to affect the rest of the parts of the body. For instance, a few sensors might go on the upper and lower lips of an object for perfect-looking talking, and maybe some more on the brows to create realistic frowns and blinks, or one for each of the parts of each finger to make it look stunningly fluid when a character moves to point at something. The infrared sensors read directly into a receiver or computer and what's recorded is where each sensor hit point A, point B, point C and so on, and when, while the human or animal was in action. Those stats are then applied to the same parts on the CG object, and the data is applied to keys at the right times. This whole process eventually tells the CG object to move in almost the most identical possible way as the real world object. The effects of this process are truly amazing.

Non-Uniform Rational B-Spline: A perpendicular, straight edged loft that is created when connecting 2 profiles.
Different solids are produced by selecting the profiles in different orders.
Lofted profiles always produce a 3-D Solid. Boolean functions, including the Round Blend and Shell feature, can be performed on Lofts but the properties cannot be changed from Solid to Surfaces.

NURBS: Short for *Non-Uniform Rational B-Spline*, a mathematical representation of a 3-D object. Most CAD/CAM applications support NURBS, which can be used to represent analytic shapes, such as cones, as well as free-form shapes, such as a car body.

onionskinning: a term that commonly refers to a graphic process in which an image or animation is composed of a couple of different layers. Imagine it as a series of totally transparent pieces of plastic with different drawings on them. When they are all stacked on top of one another, a composite is formed. This is widely used in traditional animation when the background and each character is a separate layer. This way, only layers have to be redrawn or repositioned for a new frame. Onionskinning is also found in computer software where different effects can be placed on different layers and later composited into a final image or animation.

over-the-shoulder: a shot of a person from over the shoulder of the person they are having dialogue with.

pixel: the most basic component of any computer graphic. Pixel stands for picture element. It corresponds to the smallest thing that can be drawn on a computer screen. Every computer graphic is made up of a grid of pixels. When these pixels are painted onto the screen, they form an image.

point-of-view: a shot done from the perspective of the subject.

primitives: a sphere, a box, a cylinder, a cone, or a torus. If you really look around, you might realize that many objects around you are made up of very simple objects.

production cel: the final result of creating animation using traditional ink and paint techniques, this is the art, which we see on the movie screen. Cel inkers transfer the animator's drawings onto transparent acetate sheets, and cel painters paint the character's colors on the reverse side. Each cel is then photographed against a background by a special movie film camera, typically two-film frames for each cel. The word "cel" comes from "cellulose nitrate," an early form of the acetate material used today. "Vintage Production Cel" usually refers to artwork prior to 1970. It is estimated that 95% of the production artwork created prior to 1970 was destroyed or discarded.

production drawing: an animator's drawings, which are used as the basis for creating animation cels. An "Animator's Rough" is typically very sketchy and loose, created to establish the look and emotions of a character in that particular moment. An "Extreme Drawing" is often two rough drawings that show the character at the beginning and end of a movement or action. From the Rough Drawings, "clean-up" artists refine these drawings and "fill in the blanks" between the extreme drawings (called "tweening"). Finally, when the most refined and usually precise drawings are approved, they are used to transfer the image (called "inking") onto a clear acetate cel. Usually rendered in graphite and/or colored pencil on paper, drawings illustrate an animator's creative process of bringing characters to life.

Ray trace shadow: a type of shadow effect consisting of a hard, solid shadow. Ray trace can make reflections look much more realistic and volumetric. Expect a long rendering time, because ray trace means the programs tracking the rays of the light source and applying shadows accordingly, very precisely.

rendering: the process a computer uses to create an image from a data file. Most 3-D graphics programs are not capable of drawing the whole scene on the run with all the colors, textures, lights, and shading. Instead, the user handles a mesh, which is a rough representation of an object. When the user is satisfied with the mesh, the image is then rendered.

resolution: in computer graphics either refers to the number of pixels per inch or other unit of measure (centimeter for example) on a monitor or printer. It is also sometimes used to describe the total number of pixels on a monitor. Resolution is usually measured in pixels per inch or dots per inch (dpi).
Most monitors can display at 72 dpi. Monitors come in a variety of resolutions. They can get as small as 320 pixels by 200 pixels or as large as 1280 by 1024.
Printers also can print at many different resolutions. The resolution can be as small as 128 dpi or less, to 300 dpi on inkjet printers, to 720 dpi on a laser printer, and up to 2000 dpi on high-quality typesetters.

sericel & serigraph: serigraphy, the printing term for the silk-screen process, is a fine art process in which limited editions are created by meticulously screening the colors of an image onto the back of an acetate cel or the surface of fine art paper or canvas, one color at a time. The image is separated into its individual colors, then each is transferred onto a stretched screen of silk which acts like a stencil. Inks are forced through the stretched screen onto a cel, fine art paper, or canvas, one color at a time. When all individual colors are screened onto the cel or paper, together they form the complete image. Silk-screened cels – called sericels – are typically modest in price since their edition sizes are usually large, and are not hand-signed. Limited edition serigraphs on paper or canvas are typically hand-signed by the artist indicating their personal approval of each work of art, then individually numbered to identify each work of art as a part of the total edition.

squash & stretch: an effect in which a character is taken through a series of exaggerated poses, from flattened to elongated. Stretching serves to emphasize the speed and direction of motion. Squashing highlights the effect of an abrupt change of direction or a sudden stop.

shadow maps: the opposite of ray trace. Consists of soft, fuzzy, foggy shadows to give it more of a realistic look that there is not only one light source. Faster rendering than its brother, but it can be a bit off on preciseness and can look kind of stupid if the falloff of a light source isn't just right. Shadow maps don't trace the rays, they're quickly determined by where the object is, where the light is, what its angle is, and how far away they are from each other.

sphere: a 3-D circle, a ball, if you will.

torus: basically a 3-D donut shape, like a lifesaver, or ring, or a donut. Just one of the many interesting shapes you can use.

track: the measuring window on which you place the keys of your animation. You can move keys back or forward to cut off the animation at certain, exact points, or to increase their speed.

tween: creates smooth motion between keyframes where the action is most dramatic.

wide shot: a shot that captures all of the subjects' bodies as well as much of the scenery.

About the Contributing Authors:

Vicky Jenson, Director.
Vicky Jenson graduated from the San Francisco Academy of Art and later from California State Northridge. Her career spans live action and animation. Vicky's live action short film *Family Tree*, completed in 2002, has received numerous Best Short and Audience Favorite awards. She is now directing DreamWorks' comedy, *Shark Tale*™.

Mary Ann Malcomb, Animator.
Mary Ann Malcomb received a Bachelor of Arts Degree in International Relations from the University of California at Davis and completed a three-year course of study on character animation at California Institute of the Arts.
She began her career in animation doing character layout on television series. She worked at traditional animation before her current assignment as a Computer-Generated Animator on *Shark Tale*™.

Cathy Jones, Animator.
Cathy Jones received a Bachelor of Arts Degree in Arts and Humanities from Chaffey College. She has taught animation at California Institute of the Arts. She began her career doing visual development and storyboard on a feature film and an award-winning television special.
She is working on her first computer-generated feature, *Shark Tale*™.

Claire Morrissey, Animator.
Claire Morrissey received a Bachelor of Arts Degree in Film and Communications from Sheridan College in Montreal, Canada. She began her career as an animator on commercials and feature films for major studios. She did traditional animation on the Academy Award nominated *Spirit: Stallion of the Cimarron* and is working on the computer-generated feature, *Shark Tale*™.

Michelle Cowart, Animator.
Michelle Cowart received a Bachelor of Fine Arts Degree in Computer Animation from Ringling School of Art and Design in Sarasota, Florida. She began her career as a 3-D character animator on DreamWorks' first traditionally animated feature, *The Prince of Egypt* where she animated characters and crowds. Michelle is serving as a 3-D character animator on the feature, *Shark Tale*™.

Kathy Zielinski, Animator.
Kathy Zielinski graduated from the California Institute of the Arts. She received a student academy award and a student focus award for a film she created at Cal Arts. She began her career as an animator and a character designer on feature animations for Disney. She is currently serving as an Animator on the feature, *Shark Tale*™.

Judith Love Cohen, Author.
Cohen is a Registered Professional Electrical Engineer with bachelor's and master's degrees in engineering from the University of Southern California and University of California, Los Angeles. She has written plays, screenplays, and newspaper articles, in addition to her series of children's books that began with *You Can Be a Woman Engineer.*

David Arthur Katz, Art Director.
Katz received his training in art education and holds a master's degree from the University of South Florida where he specialized in animation. His most recent animation, Cartoon Sea, has been in numerous film festivals and played on many PBS stations. His early animations and children's book illustrations have been acquired and shown in a number of museums across the country.

Acknowledgements

DreamWorks' Shark Tale and all characters and elements from DreamWorks' Shark Tale are the property of DreamWorks, L.L.C. and are used with the express permission of DreamWorks, L.L.C.

Special thanks to Michael Vollman, Fumi Kitahara, and Wendy Backe at DreamWorks, L.L.C.

Photography by Stacey Halper.

Nomenclature by Jason Peters, animator.